MEDITATIONS FOR TODDLERS WHO DO TOO MUCH

Sarah Gillespie and Nancy Parent

Andrews and McMeel
A Universal Press Syndicate Company
Kansas City

ISBN: 0-8362-2159-1

Library of Congress Catalog Card Number: 96-84005

Book design by Top Dog Design

ATTENTION: SCHOOLS AND BUSINESSES
Andrews and McMeel books are available at quantity discounts with bulk purchase for educational, business, or sales promotional use. For information, please write to: Special Sales Department, Andrews and McMeel, 4520 Main Street, Kansas City, Missouri 64111.

For little boys named Howard,
past and present.

I LOVE YOU, YOU LOVE ME, WE'RE A HAPPY FAMILY

A cheerful face makes for love.
—Orhot Tsadikim

The affirmation of *I* in I love you is, indeed and in creed, an affirmation of self. So, if I love you and I am Barney, do I not, in reality—in *deed*—love myself? But if I am Barney, am I not also a purple dinosaur? Is that who I love—is that after all who we *all* love? But why shouldn't I love that dinosaur? If not me, then who, Baby Bop? And therefore shouldn't I then, loving myself, loving the very Barneyness of me, listen to the damn song over and over and over again . . .

GOD BLESS MOMMY, DADDY, AND APPLE JUICE

All the speed is in the morning
—Alice Harvey

To awaken in the morning and sing with the birds. . . . Yes, it is morning and yes, we will have our apple juice. Isn't that, in its entirety, the meaning? Do we need more? We love Mommy, and she brings us apple juice. We love Daddy, he refills our bottle of apple juice. And we love, for its coolness and its richness, and most of all its sugar, sugar, sugarness, we love our apple juice. More, we say, we want more, more apple juice. And it really is okay.

God Grant Me the Serenity to Hold It Until I Can Get to the Potty

I thought I would love the potty. When Mommy sat on it, I said, that will be me someday. I, too, will sit on that porcelain throne. When Daddy stood at it, I thought, me too. Water, water everywhere. I too will shoot water into the bowl someday. But now there is no shooting of water, no sitting on cold thrones, now there is only the urge to go, and what do they mean by holding it? Hold it where? Hold it how? I use my hand but it doesn't help. Where is the potty? Quick, where is the potty? Or at least a diaper?

A DAY WITHOUT CHEERIOS IS LIKE A DAY WITHOUT SUNSHINE

The man who causes himself pain by not enjoying what is not sinful may be called a sinner.
—The Talmud

I t's the crunch, we all know that. But we must accept it, the crunch of Cheerios, the deeply satisfying oaty O's, that is what we crave. That is what we must have. And, though no addiction is good, might not this one be okay? At least until we hit maybe five or so?

THE TERRIBLE TWOS— A RITE OF PASSAGE

Life is full of passages. I will grow, I will graduate, I will marry and raise children. But for today, I will be two years old. And that means I will have my tantrums, declare my selfness, cry out to the world "I am here and I am two. You got a problem with that?" And it means I will be extremely obnoxious. Because I'm asserting my independence. Because I am testing the limits. Because, well, because I'm two and hey, it's my turn.

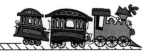

WHY SAY YES WHEN IT'S SO MUCH MORE FUN TO SAY NO

My mantra for today . . . my mantra for the next two years—"NO." It is the tongue hitting the top of the palate that makes the word so vivid. The strong "O" (is there a relationship to Cheerio here?). Cheeri-NO's? I guess not, *no*, there is no relationship to Cheerios. *No, no, no*—repeat it many times, the tongue tickles, the mind numbs, the mom capitulates. It is a good word, this *no*. "Just say *no*"—some woman, some goddess in a red dress said that—and she was right. *No* is good, *no* is complete, *no* is so much better, so very much better than yes.

IF I CAN'T SAY IT,
I'LL JUST BITE IT!

Let dogs delight to bark and bite
For God hath made them so . . .

—Isaac Watts, *Against*
Quarreling and Fighting

I know its name, I think I heard it in play group, but I can't say it. I see what I want, I can hold it in my hand, but what the heck is the word for it? Clearly, it's mine—because everything is mine—but what is it called? I open my mouth wide, wider, widest. And chomp, chew, who needs words, anyway? I can talk with my teeth.

MINE, MINE, MINE

Children and fools want everything.
—George Savile,
Marquess of Halfax

It's a waking-up-in-the-morning song. Mine, mine, mine. It's a go-to-sleep-at-night song. Mine, mine, mine. It's the song that gets me through a long day of errands, play group, napping, and finger-painting. Mine, mine, mine. It's the song I sing to my day-care pals. Mine, mine, mine. Siblings want a chance at the Duplos? I think not. They're mine, mine, mine. All mine. Ever mine. Everything is mine. Leave it alone whatever it is, because once I set eyes on it, it's *mine!*

I KNOW YOU THINK THAT YOU'RE IN CHARGE

Children begin by loving their parents.
After a time they judge them.
Rarely, if ever, do they forgive them.
— Oscar Wilde, *A Woman
of No Importance*

Yes, you're bigger, we can see that. But that does not mean you're better, or even stronger. For instance, if I lay down on the floor in the middle of the supermarket and let go with one of my screams (and how piercing is *your* scream these days?) you may have the brute strength to pick me up—but who won the moment? So many adults these days are searching for their inner child. Who needs to search, who needs an inner child, when you are like me, all child? Yes, I am child, I am toddler child—inner, outer, over, under—I am child and I am clearly in charge.

I SCREAM, YOU SCREAM, WE ALL SCREAM . . . FOR ABSOLUTELY ANYTHING

Noise is undomesticated music.
—Ambrose Bierce

Perhaps I will grow up to be Luciano Pavarotti or Alice Cooper. It's too soon to say, too early to tell. But if I don't begin practicing now, I'll take a backseat to some early achieving screamer whose parents never said, "Stop already. That's enough." And it never really is enough. That's why I continue to scream. I scream for today and on into tomorrow. I scream because I love the sound of screaming. I scream because I'm a kid and it just feels like the thing to do.

And the voice of the child is heard throughout the land.

IF WE NEEDED SHOES AND SOCKS, WE WOULD HAVE BEEN BORN WITH THEM

Only the wearer knows where the shoe pinches.
—English proverb

Remember when I was born and you looked at my teeny little toes and said they were so sweet and beautiful? Well, it hasn't been that long and they're still not half bad. So why cover them up with shoes and socks ? I only started walking a little while ago (remember?) and I need to feel the floor beneath these little piggies for balance, not to mention security. So who needs shoes, who needs socks? Look at it this way, I'll just grow out of one and lose the other anyway. They're not worth the time, believe me.

Meditations on Day Care

Breathe in and out and visualize it. Ten kids, one adult. Sharing toys with other kids, sharing quiet time, sharing ear infections. Daaaay Caaaarre, make it a chant, a chant that says with any luck, Mom and Dad will pick me up before the teacher goes home leaving me to starve here alone. Daaaay Caaaarre, a chant that says maybe this week the snack will not involve bananas or graham crackers. Daaaay Caaaarre, where the naps are always at the same time, but then, so is lunch. Daaaay Caaaarre, it may not be perfect but it's better than woooorkkk.

ET TU, MOMMY?

*A baby is an angel whose wings
decrease as his legs increase.*
—French proverb

Hello? It's me, the cute one, remember me? Remember how you'd walk me in your arms at night until I fell asleep? Remember how warm and mushy you got the first time I held my teeny, tiny little arms out to you, my mom, my very own Mommy? Remember that? Remember when nothing I could do was wrong? Remember when you called me your precious little angel? Right, I remember it too. So what happened? Lately you have been all over me. First it's say this word, say that word. What do you think I am, a parrot? Then it's brush your teeth, pick up your toys, sit on the potty. Used to be all I had to do to please you was roll over. Now it's walk, talk, brush, poop. So Mom, let's take a deep breath and then say after me, "Today I'll leave the kid alone."

THE SOUL'S MUSIC

Never hate a song that has sold a half-million copies.
—Irving Berlin
speaking to Cole Porter

Why does music move us so? Is it the soaring unity of the instruments, the awe of the creative genius able to bring such beauty into being, or is it simply the blend of voice and instrument which fills our hearts with such joy? Perhaps it is best not to analyze. For now let us say it is better just to accept. Accept the melody, the harmony, the music itself as we sing together, loudly and with feeling, annoyingly and with pride, over and over and over again, *"The wheels on the bus go 'round and 'round, all through the town!"*

CLOTHES UP

From the cradle to the coffin, underwear comes first.
—Bertolt Brecht

When we think about it, what are clothes, really? Artifice. Cover-ups. Masquerade costumes that hide the true person, the true child, the true toddler. And so, today I will say good-bye to clothes. Today I will feel the breeze of the department store air-conditioning on my bare behind. Today, the minute you turn your back, I will know what it is to be fully, totally free of all bounds, free of all bindings, free of zippers, snaps, and Velcro. And if, when this overwhelming urge, this human need, this siren's song occurs to me while we're picking up frozen green beans at the ShopWell, I say so be it. And if my nature dictates nudity as soon as we enter Grandma's house (she thinks you don't supervise me anyway), I say—so be it. No matter how sweet that new outfit is, nothing is sweeter than taking it off. And I will, just for today, I will.

ATTENTION MUST BE PAID

Where there is no jealousy there is no love.
—German proverb

Excuse me? Hello? This is your kid speaking. I hate to be nosy and you know that I'm not overly possessive, but just who is it that you think you're talking to? Who is that child on which you are bestowing praise, conversation, and all of your attention? No wait, I misspoke, it's not *your* attention, it's *my* attention. For if you are paying attention to some other kid, you're not paying attention to *me!* And that is, after all, what you're here for. I'll just move to your side, in case you forgot who your first and only love is. Maybe I'll grab hold of your skirt—you know I get insecure around strangers—and suck my thumb while looking longingly up at you. Not working. Okay. I'll up the ante a bit, here you go, the tears are coming, the sniffling is starting. I think I've got you back, you're looking at me with irritation but at least you're looking. I'll try a shy smile, bat my lashes a bit, and if the kid's not outta here in twenty seconds, I'll throw a fit. It is only me you love, isn't it?

PET PEEVES

The dog was created specially for children.
He is the god of frolic
—Henry Ward Beecher, *Proverbs*
from Plymouth Pulpit

Ooh, look, look, it's a doggy. Ooh, let go, let me pet the doggy. Nice doggy, nice doggy. Ooh, look at the doggie's tail, it is wagging. Let me touch the doggie's tail. Nice doggy, nice doggy. Does the tail stay attached when you pull it? It does! Nice doggy, nice doggy. Ooh, look at the doggie's eyes, they are brown and big and soulful. Ooh let me touch the doggie's eye with my finger, ooh doggy pulled away. Nice doggy, nice doggy. Ooh, listen to the doggy talk. What a nice low sound. Like thunder. Grrrrrrrrrrrrrrr. Nice doggy, nice doggy? Ooh, look at the doggie's teeth, the doggy is smiling and showing me all of his teeth. Nice doggy, nice doggy. Ooh look at Mommy run, she hasn't moved that fast in six months. Wheeeeeee, Mommy is picking me up. Nice Mommy, nice Mommy.

CLIMB EVERY FOUNTAIN

(with feeling)

Climb every fountain,
See every saw,
Dig up every sandbox,
Till you've tried them all.

Swing every swing set,
Balance every beam,
Slide down every slider,
Till you find your dream

A park that will have,
The best gym stuff in town,
No one else can join in,
Till you want them around!

Climb every fountain,
See every saw,
Dig up every sandbox,
Till you've tried them all.

I WON'T WAIT, DON'T ASK ME

What do you mean, "There will be a ten-minute wait"? Perhaps you didn't notice me here, the short one clinging to my father's knee? Think of it as a mathematical equation—how many minutes have there been in my toddler life, and how many have there been in your adult life? To me, you see, ten minutes is a much larger percentage of my life. Or, you can look at it another way. I'm a toddler, I'm hungry, I'm bored, and if I have to wait a full ten minutes in order to be seated in one of your restaurant's spaghetti-stained booster seats, there's no counting the amount of havoc I will have to wreak. I'll start small, with a cry, "Daaaadddyyy, I'm hunnnggrrryy" (see the hostess glance nervously around the dining room). Next a quick run down the aisle, ducking the lady with the tray of hot soup (her balance isn't all it could be). Then a scream as Dad grabs my collar (the hostess is turning pale) and sure enough, aren't we lucky? A table has opened up for us and we've been moved to the head of the line. How nice. Thanks so much. With service like this, you know we'll be back.

GOOD MORNING, WORLD

'Tis always morning somewhere in the world!
—Richerd Hengest Horne, *Orion*

hy are we supposed to like the morning? Yes, it's nice that it's daylight out, but it's also nice right here in my bed. Warm and cozy with my blanket and Teddy. The sun may be up, but I am not. It's an unhappy conundrum all right, that the only thing I hate worse than going to sleep at night is waking up in the morning. I hear Mommy grabbing a shower before getting me up. Daddy sticks his head in my door. He comes over and picks me up—yuck, his breath smells awful and he has little hairs on his chin that weren't there last night. I squirm and whine. He puts me down. Good morning, my foot. Why are we supposed to like morning? I don't like morning. Not today, in any case. And embracing that fact, knowing I don't like morning, and I don't have to like morning I can roll over once more and close my eyes. And for today, that is enough.

SEND IN THE CLOWNS

Being a child is in itself a profession.
—Clifton Fadiman

Guess who's coming to my birthday party. Is it a clown, is it a magician, is it a lady with a pony I can ride, is it Barney or the Power Rangers or Big Bird? Maybe it's all of them. Because, if Alexander had pony rides and Jason had a magician, I have to have at least a clown . . . a really good clown who can do balloon tricks and who comes with his own rabbit. Otherwise how am I going to compete? Two years old and I'm already on the slow track—a party with cake and ice cream only? Please, I may be short and still in diapers but I have my pride. But what if there is no clown, no pony for photo ops, no magician, no Barney? I guess worse things could happen. It won't be so bad, really. I can learn to accept this failure of parenting! I can lower my expectations. And besides, it'll make a good story when I go into therapy a few years from now. Right, Mommy?

BABY SINGS THE BLUES

What is it about holding my breath that is so deeply satisfying. Is it that filled-up feeling and the tingle in my toes? Perhaps it's the dizzy, woozy lightness in my head. Perhaps it's the color itself; blue is, after all, the color of serenity. No, the satisfaction of holding my breath until I turn blue as the summer sky is quite simple. It's watching the look of stubborn parenting gradually melt off of Mommy's face to be replaced by a look of resignation and the offer of a cookie. I don't say yes right away, though I do exhale. I let her wait until the color returns to my cheeks before I say the word, "Cookie?" Yes, cookie, Mommy gives me a cookie, and I ask the question I've asked myself hundred of times before, "What is it about a cookie that is so deeply satisfying?" I don't know, but I'll hold my breath all day long to get one.

BOOGERS

Vulgarity is simply the conduct of other people.
—Oscar Wilde,
An Ideal Husband

Yes, I know what people say. It's a vulgar habit, one I must quickly learn to outgrow. But not now. Not for today. For aren't there worse habits? Won't I have to avoid so many in my just-starting-out lifetime? So now, for today, it is important that I know, that I explore, that I discover for myself with all the joy of my youth, the magic that is my nose. The outside I know, I caress that smooth-skinned side while sucking my thumb or fondling my blanket. But that warm, moist inner sanctum, that is what I must explore. The boogers that live there, that I can bring into daylight on the tip of my finger to roll, to taste (salty as a soft pretzel), to examine, to embrace. Like warm Play Doh, like the softest Silly Putty. Boogers, yet another part of the wonder that is me.

SOAP GETS IN YOUR EYES

Shampoo. The word itself sounds evil. First, there's sham—meaning a fake, a falsehood, not worthy of innocent youth. And Poo, isn't that what is now in my diaper that Mommy wants to see in the toilet? Shampoo. It's not much of a word, and it's an even worse mantra. But we mustn't be negative, we must learn to embrace even life's worst moments—for what they give us, for what we learn. From Shampoo I have learned that life is a series of circles.

> I hate it when my eyes sting.
> Shampoo stings when it gets in my eyes.
> Stinging eyes make me cry.
> When I cry my eyes sting.
> I hate it when my eyes sting.
> The circle of life. You gotta accept it.

STOP ME IF YOU'VE
HEARD THIS ONE

Laughter is the corrective force which stops us from being cranks.
—Henri Bergson

There's nothing like getting a laugh. Sometimes all I have to do is make a face and, bingo, I've got the room in the palm of my teeny, tiny hand. Now that I can talk, I'm even better. Like when I mispronounce words. Pizgetti. That's what I call those noodles with red sauce. The first time I said it, I thought my mother was going to faint, she laughed so hard. When Daddy came home she made him listen to me before he could take his tie off. Tell Daddy what's for dinner. Pizgetti, I said, and he roared. So it's funny, I know that. That's why I say it all the time. Pizgetti, pizgetti, pizgetti. My theory is you go with a formula that works. Would Letterman get rid of the Top 10 lists? Not even for the Academy Awards. So I say, if the folks like my saying Pizgetti, hey, I give it to 'em. It's a family thing. A bonding moment. They don't laugh so much anymore, sometimes they pretend they didn't hear me. I figure they just want me to say it louder. PIZGETTI, I shout, PIZGETTI. "That's enough, now," Mommy says. "We heard you the first time," says Dad. PIZGETTI, PIZGETTI, PIZGETTI. I can say it all night, or at least until I get a laugh.

WHAT'S THE RUSH?

We're always rushing, it seems. And for what? To get to work? To get to day care? To do the laundry, shopping, and cleaning? Get a haircut, cook the dinner, have the meeting, fill the car up. All of it in a rush. Well, I ask, "What's the rush?" I say stop and smell the roses. And while I'm sniffing the buds, I'll stop and play with my "See 'n' Say," sing a few rounds of "Wheels on the Bus," watch a Barney tape, read a book. You want me to brush my teeth? Sure. I want to please. So I'll brush my teeth just as soon as I watch another tape, read another book, sing all three hundred choruses of "This Old Man," and then, then, I'll brush my teeth. Slowly. Because teeth are important and you can't learn to take care of them too early. So I'll slowly, tooth by tooth brush my teeth. Because life flies by too fast. And because it doesn't really matter if you're a little late for work again, does it?

LOVE

Whoever cares to learn will always find a teacher.
—German proverb

Love, the poet says, makes the world go 'round. Well, today my world is going 'round and 'round and 'round. Because now I know what love is. Now I celebrate love. Love is, and I know this with all my heart, love is what I feel for my day-care teacher. As we pull up to day care every morning I get nervous about leaving Mommy, and I won't let go of Daddy's hand. But just as my little face begins to crumble and I start to whimper, Miss Ellen appears at the door of our room. She's a lot like Mommy but she's not as bossy. And she never gets tired. She smiles almost all of the time, and makes sure snacks and lunch are right on schedule. She never tells me to stop pulling at her because she had a lousy day at the office. I *am* her office. Every time I do an art project she writes on it, "For Mommy" or "For Daddy." How can I tell her that everything I do is really for "Miss Ellen"? Does she feel the same way about me? When we all leave at night and she stays behind, to wait by herself in that little room for us to return, does she sit down at the table, in my chair, her cute but tremendous knees under her chin, and think about me?

RISE AND SHINE

The childhood shows the man,
As morning shows the day.
—John Milton,
Paradise Regained

Aren't mornings great? Despite my full diaper, I feel fresh and sunny and ready for a great day. Come on, Mom. Hurry up, Dad. It's morning and it's time to get up! I love this big-kid bed that I can get out of all on my own. It makes me feel so grown-up, it makes me feel so powerful, it makes me feel like coming into your room and telling you, "It's morning, it's a bright new morning, and it's time to rise and shine." This moment requires noise and running and jumping and laughing and opening your bedroom door and bringing in the morning sunshine with me. Yes, it's Sunday. Yes, it's only 5:30. But you gotta agree, it's some beautiful morning.

LATER IS ALWAYS TOO LATE

Are we having fun yet?
—Bill Griffith,
Zippy the Pinhead

L ife is full of laters. Later, you can have ice cream. Later, you can go swimming. Later, you can play with Daddy. Later, you can do anything you want. But not now, not today. Why is it that later is always a lifetime away?

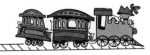

A Meditation on Mommy

The warmest bed of all is mother's.
—The Talmud

My Mom is the best, she likes to eat out.
She washes the dishes and tries not to pout,
When Dad tells the neighbors how much he helps out.

True, two times a week he takes out the trash,
And explains after payday why we're still short on cash,
But Mom takes her paycheck and goes to the store,
And picks up the groceries, dry cleaning, and more.
She takes me for check-ups, holds my head when I'm sick,
After Dad swings me up in the air way too quick.

So we'll march through the arches,
McDonald's displays,
And give Mom a hand while she carries our trays,
Full of the best that old Ron has to offer,
'Cause this is my Mom and I think she's a whopper.

UNITED THEY STAND

*Parents were invented to make children happy
by giving them something to ignore.*
—Ogden Nash

Lately, I've been thinking about fairness. Sharing is fair, that's what we're told—one for me and one for you is a concept I am all too often reminded of. Yet, and here is the problem, here is the philosophical conundrum we, at least I, face daily. Why do Mom and Dad think that two against one is fair? For example—I want to go to the park, Mom and Dad want to go to the supermarket. Who wins? You bet, we go buy a ton of groceries. It's not fair, I say. It's not fair, I scream. The response, if I get a response, is that "life is not fair." I know that, but explain to me again why I have to be fair and share my toys when life, it seems, doesn't.

SORRY, WRONG NUMBER

I love the telephone. I love to hold the receiver to my ear and hear people talk. Sometimes they even say my name! Communication is a wonderful thing and I am happy to do my part, to listen while people talk to me on the telephone. But Mommy's always whispering in my ear. Can't she see that I'm busy? "Say, 'Hi, Grampa.'" she whispers. Why should I say "Hi, Grampa?" He knows I'm there, he's talking to me. "Are you being good?" he asks. I nod my head. Communication can take many forms, not all of them vocal, Mom. You should know that by now. I love the telephone. Really I do. I just have my own way of using it.

SHYNESS

There is nothing wrong with feeling shy. Shyness is a fault only if you don't get what you want. But for me, shyness gets me exactly what I want. What might I want? you ask. Attention would be nice. A grown-up's smile, the offer of a sweet treat, a pat on the head. Little things, but pleasant ones. But if I hide behind you when we go into a new situation, let me. I'm a little frightened, a little shy, and a little aware that shyness works. I know what I'm doing—trust me on this one. Yes, for today I'm shy. But for today I'm also perfectly content to be just that way.

IT'S ALWAYS SOMETHING

No one is so busy as the man who has nothing to do.
—French proverb

There are those who say a toddler's life is all fun and games. It is our lot in life, it seems, to play the innocent, the clown, the baby. And so I have to ask myself, "Is life all fun and games? Is it really as easy to swallow as a McDonald's Happy Meal—and just as full-filling? Does a toddler not think? Does a toddler not worry? If you prick a toddler, does he or she not get a boo-boo? No, a toddler's life isn't all fun and games—there are meaningless rules to obey. There are play dates to dress for, younger kids to put up with till you can grab their toys away. There are parents to please and appease (why can't they be happy with themselves so they can then be happy with me?). And there are experiments to perform—if a lamp breaks and Mommy doesn't hear it, did a lamp really break? It's a busy life, and for today, it's mine.

KARMA CENTRAL

It is dangerous to confuse children with angels.
—Sir David Maxwell Fyfe

When we analyze the meaning of "Isn't she just adorable?" we find that the seemingly innocuous phrase is full of ambiguity and harm. First of all, there's "Isn't she"—beginning a sentence with a negative can't be a good idea, at least not if the sentence refers to me. "Just" meaning only, meaning mere, meaning not very much. And finally, "adorable," from the verb, "to adore"—to adulate, look up to, to love. Well, adorable is all right, I guess. Even so, I do not feel like being adorable today. And even so, even when I pout and stick my lower lip out as far as it will go, still the people in the supermarket, the mall, the bank persist, "Isn't she adorable?" they say, over and over again. It's just my karma I guess.

FASHION TIPS

Good clothes open all doors.
—Thomas Fuller

Getting dressed is my favorite part of the morning. As with all things worthwhile, there are steps to becoming fashionable. *Step one* is contemplation—what to wear, what to wear? This is an important step and should never be rushed, even by Mommy, who needs to get you fed and to day care before she goes to work. *Step two* is underwear. Clearly toilet training helps here since it's much easier to slip on a pair of panties than it is to wait for Daddy to finish shaving and dressing so that he can diaper while you cry and drool all over his dark blue suit. *Step three* is decision-making, try the red shirt and the purple pants, the orange and yellow-striped shorts and the floral cotton blouse, or perhaps a dress directly over your pajamas—a bit outré, but it works. *Step four,* change. *Step five,* change. *Step six,* cry as Mommy yells. *Step seven,* change. *Step eight,* socks—matching pairs is for babies, go for broke here. *Step nine,* shoes—select a clearly inappropriate but fabulous pair like water shoes instead of snow boots; it could work. *Step ten,* insist on putting the shoes on yourself. *Step eleven,* cry as Daddy yells. Step twelve, refer to step four.

MY, MYSELF AND JEREMY

Imagination is the beginning of creation.
—George Bernard Shaw

There is nothing imaginary about Jeremy. He is invisible, this I grant you, but to dismiss a friend, a companion, a fellow toddler as imaginary simply because he doesn't exist is absolutely barbaric. Jeremy is my friend. Although he's highly verbal he allows me to do most of the talking. Sometimes we sing together, Jeremy and I—he takes harmony and I cover melody. Jeremy likes to sleep over (although we don't discuss it, I get the feeling his home life isn't a happy one) and he's always welcome. When I wake up in the middle of the night we talk and play and sometimes sing a round or two of "Itsy Bitsy Spider." My parents think my friend is a cute aberration of my toddlerhood. I know differently. Jeremy, I know for sure, will be with me for life.

THE MEANING OF IT ALL

I am sure that books are good and I certainly share the taste of my peers. (Who among us hasn't wept at the end of *The Runaway Bunny*? Clichéd, yes. Overlauded, perhaps. But so very moving in its simplicity. Kind of like *Bridges of Madison County* for kids.) What I don't understand are the books by Penelope Leach and Dr. Spock and those *What to Expect When Your Kid Is Twenty-Five* people. Shelves full of books on how to deal with your toddler. Who says toddlers need to be dealt with? I think we're doing just fine. The other matter that needs to be addressed is, why aren't there books for toddlers on how to deal with their parents? I would like to know how to handle their periods of extreme exhaustion, their short tempers, mood swings, and antisocial glares (seen most often in restaurants and shopping malls). But I have learned that it doesn't help to gripe. If you're not part of the solution, you're part of the problem! So, I have a plan. As soon as I learn how to read and write, I'm starting work on my book, *Raising Your Parents, the Toddler Years*.

FRENCH FRIES ARE MY LIFE

*Better to have bread and an onion
with peace than stuffed fowl with strife.*
—Arab proverb

The waitress smiles and hands Mom the kiddy menu as Dad struggles to get me into the embarrassing and uncomfortable booster seat. I play with the blobs of congealed ketchup on my "own special seat" and wait for the verdict. Will it be a "Little Boy Blue" peanut butter and (blue-grape) jelly sandwich or maybe the "Anchors Aweigh" fish sticks? Whatever we choose will be accompanied by those universal standards of kids' meals—soggy french fries. Ever wonder why we cover them in ketchup? It's to cut the grease. Not that I mind them, really. In fact, I love them. It's more the assumption I resent. I'm a toddler, therefore I like greasy french fries.

FRIENDSHIP

Friends are born, not made.
—Henry Adams

So often we take our friends for granted. Yet, what would we do without that special someone we can ignore, whose toys we can grab, whose attention we can resent? Friendship is a wonderful thing; it's something to be treasured. Who else but a friend would shout *mine, mine, mine* really loudly in your face when all you want to do is take a look at her new tricycle? Who else but a friend would bite you on the arm because, out of idle curiosity, you grab hold of his airplane and refuse to give it back? We are reminded of the old but still so true rhyme: make new friends, but keep the old. One is silver and the other's gold. Yes, friends are wonderful—and whether golden or silver, they always have a neat plastic toy worth grabbing.

HOLD THAT POSE

Why do parents feel that every move is worth a picture? I wear a new outfit . . . take a picture. I take a bath . . . take a picture. I meet with Santa . . . take a picture. Sometimes I feel like one admittedly adorable photo op. It was worse, of course, before my sister was born. Between chasing me and changing her, the Kodak moments seem to have slowed down a bit. The worst is the department store photo, where a creepy guy with pimples and hot dog breath tries to make me laugh. Why should I laugh? This photograph is a diminishment of me—does anyone believe I actually own that little red wagon? I would like to own that wagon, for a moment I think I do. And I smile. Flash goes the lightbulb, click goes the camera, away goes the wagon. Wait, I thought that was mine. Bring back my wagon. I'll be good, I promise. But as Mom drags me away in tears I understand. The wagon isn't mine. It's only a prop, a concept I should be too young to grasp.

QUALITY TIME

So often we look to our parents for answers they cannot give, such as, why is the sky blue. Or why does Daddy, who knows everything, have such a tough time figuring out how to put together my new tricycle. But what I want to know, the question that plagues my day-care day is, what *is* quality time? I know it's supposed to be that special time that Mom and Dad spend with me. Fine so far. But who decided that quality time has to occur just when I'm getting ready to curl up with a good Thomas video, or when I'm deeply involved with my Legos. Why is that the time we suddenly have to go to the Children's Museum (admittedly, their Lego display is awesome) or read a book together or make cookies? These are all activities I enjoy, I admit, but do they have to interfere with the quality time I spend with myself?

ICE CREAM

*I doubt whether the world holds for anyone a more soul-stirring
surprise than the first adventure with ice-cream.*

—Heywood Broun
Holding a Baby

The trick is to let it melt a little before you start eating it. As the
first silky stream of melting ice cream hits your hand (important,
too, is the cone, the brown one with the pointy bottom is easier to drop).
Begin to lick. Ooooh. It's cold and creamy and sweet. The best flavor is
vanilla, although if you're strictly interested in the parent-irritation-factor
and the ice-cream mustache, go for chocolate. The brown is more authen-
tic on the upper lip and the chocolate stain is harder to get out of clothes.
Try getting your nose into the cone as you continue licking, it's adorable
and it makes you sneeze disgusting-looking stuff. As you near the middle
of the cone, let it tip toward the floor. Try to do this without your parent
seeing, so that you are not reprimanded until the ice cream falls to the
floor and you are crying. At this point, odds are that you'll get a new cone.
Simple mathematics show that if you've already eaten half and you get
another entire cone, you're a half cone ahead. Go with it, go for it, it's
worth the effort, it really is, because, after all, we're talking ice cream.

ME, MYSELF AND I, I, I

*To love oneself is the beginning
of a life-long romance.*
—Oscar Wilde,
An Ideal Husband

Who, pray tell, is that gorgeous individual in the mirror? Who, give us a hint, is that adorable toddler whose reflection gleams from the toy store window? Me, that's who it is. Me, Me, Me. Look at the faces I can make, so funny, so enchanting, so never-been-seen-before. Look at the hair, so shiny, so bright, so toss-my-head-and-see-how-it-moves. Look at the teeth; okay, maybe we'll skip the teeth. Look at those eyes, so sharp, so knowing, so twinkling. Let's face it, never in the entire history of this world has there been a Me. So appreciate me while you can. I know I do.

DO THAT, MOMMY

Sometimes, as a toddler, it becomes difficult to accept that we are, for the most part, small. There are times when we need to express the largeness of ourselves, to focus upon our ability to lead and to—dare we say it—control. And that is when we play games. "Follow me," we say to Mommy, "and do whatever I say. Follow me, and do whatever I do." Perhaps there are times we play too rough. "Do this, Mommy. What do you mean that hurts? That gentle slap to the face, the head, and various body parts indistinguishable from each other? Do that, Mommy. Sit where I sit, even though your behind is four sizes larger than mine. Jump up onto the chair without removing any of the toys; squeeze through the window of my yellow plastic playhouse; go headfirst over the back of the sofa; wriggle around underneath the dining room table, then pick all the crumbs out of the carpet and eat them." Actually, being little is pretty good fun. And for today, that is enough.

GO AWAY, MOMMY

*The first half of our lives is ruined by our parents
and the second half by our children.*
—Clarence Darrow

Being a toddler isn't as easy as it may seem. It is impossible to live up to parental expectations *and* listen to "Where Is Thumbkin" *and* play with Legos *and* color *and* read a book. So sometimes we have to ignore the pleading, the constant drain on our time. "Isn't it enough that I'm clean?" we say, "Do I really need a diaper? Isn't it enough that I'm cute, now you want to clip my toenails, too? Isn't it enough that I can entertain myself for five minutes? Do I really need to get dressed, brush my teeth, and put on my shoes? Go 'way, Mommy. Go 'way, until I can do all these things *myself*. Go 'way and get me some juice!"

SAY WHAT YOU MEAN!

A tart temper never mellows with age.
—Washington Irving

Don't say da-da when you mean blanket. I'm an intelligent young person, I don't need condescending names for my playthings. Do not talk down or coo at me. Treat me as the almost-adult (those seventeen years will go by in a snap) I am. A blanket is a blanket is a blanket. And if you can't handle that, I'll just start packing. As soon as I find my da-da.

A TODDLER'S ABCS

 is for accepting. "No, really, I *like* creamed turkey."

 is for belligerent. "This is *my* television."

 is for cunning. "I won't eat the Gummy Bears, I just want to carry the bag."

 is for dependent. "Are you awake, Mommy?"

 is for energetic. "I don't need to take a nap."

 is for funny. "Here's a riddle I'll bet you've never heard . . ."

 is for grumpy. "I probably should have taken a nap."

 is for huggable. "Time for bed, now."

 is for independent. "I can do it myself."

is for jealous. "I'm gonna have a little *what?*"

 is for kingly. "Push my stroller over there."

 is for lovable. "I'm cute even in Sears photos."

 is for mulish. "But I don't want my picture taken."

 is for narcissistic. "What other kids?"

 is for oversensitive. "You *yelled* at me."

 is for pushy. "*My* blocks, *my* bike, *my* world."

 is for quick. "Daddy, where are you?"

 is for rambunctious. "Let's play some more."

is for silly. "Tickle me again."

 is for temperamental. "I'm not your friend."

 is for unruly. "Give it to me, it's mine."

 is for vocal. "Because I want to."

 is for winsome. "I wish everybody could be like Barney."

 is for xenophobic. "Don't be handing me off to any strangers, Mom!"

 is for yawns. "But I'm not sleepy."

 is for zoom. "Look, Mommy, I'm an airplane."

DON'T RUSH ME!

And then the whining schoolboy with his satchel
And shining morning face, creeping like a snail
Unwillingly to school
—William Shakespeare

I am terribly busy and I've got lots more to do before we leave. There are toys here I haven't played with since I was two and a half. I have books to read, videos to watch, and songs to sing. Always remember, just because you're ready and waiting at the door, doesn't mean I am. In fact, I'm not ready at all. Hey, let's play a new game, try and catch me! When we're done with that, I'll still have to brush my teeth, put on my pants, tie my shoes, and find my jacket. So hurry up and wait just a doggone minute! Find your serenity, go with the flow, don't sweat it, don't check your watch, and always, always remember, I'm a toddler. I was born to dawdle!

I WANT SOMETHING ELSE!

*The life of children, as much as that of intemperate man,
is wholly governed by their desires.*

—Aristotle

Strapped into a car seat, sitting alone in the back of the car, staring at an empty juice container and a full trash bag, it's hard to believe you expect me to allow this without a struggle. First of all, the strap is too tight. Who invented these things, the Marquis de Sade? I can't breathe; you're cutting off my circulation. That's better. Now I can't see a thing unless you count Daddy's thinning hair as something worth staring at. The view really stinks from back here. Try it sometime and see what I mean. And who picked out that music? You say that was The Loving Spoonful? Well, you may love them but I sure don't. I don't even like them. Where's my sing-along tape? And my blanket—no, not that one, the one that I left in my room. Do me a favor and hand me that toy on the floor over there. That one. The one you can't possibly reach. Get it for me. How about my snacks? And some juice. I don't care if you're driving, I'm riding!

THE ART OF EATING

A mother never gets hit with a custard pie . . . never.
—Mack Sennett

Cereal, milk, and bananas. The seeds of creativity can be anywhere—in the yogurt on my overalls, in the apple-sauce in my hair, even in the cracker crumbs on the rug. Look, I can finger-paint with milk! And if I wave the spoon around, I can splash the wall and see if the mashed potatoes dribble down to the floor. Quiet, please, little Jackson Pollack is creating. Watch what happens when I turn the bowl upside down. Look, Mommy, it's a bowl and a hat! Wow, the floor is really wet but we don't need paper towels, I can clean it up all by myself. My pajamas are very absorbent.

LISTEN UP

Children have never been very good at
listening to their elders,
but they have never failed to imitate them.

—James Baldwin, "Fifth Avenue,
Uptown," *Nobody Knows
My Name*

Hey, guys, did you ever hear of reflective listening? Listen to me! What am I really saying here? You just think I'm hysterical, but I am actually communicating with you. So look past the crying and the shrieking, and the breast-beating, and let's hear your scenario. Or better yet, mirror what I'm doing. Go ahead. Stomp around. Kick your feet, scream your lungs out, pull your hair. It's a great release for that pent-up tension and frustration! Go ahead, try it! You'll get a lot of attention!

ON BOO-BOOS & BUMPS

I can't imagine life without the Boo-Boo Bear. It does the trick for bumps and cuts and scrapes. Even though it's always too cold against my skin, and I won't let it near my body, just seeing that trusty blue wrap helps the pain go away. Sometimes I even sleep with the Boo-Boo Bear, just for the heck of it. If everyone had a Boo-Boo Bear, the world would definitely be a better place. Boo-Boo Bear, never leave me.

WRESTLING WITH THE CAR SEAT

The car trip can draw the family together,
as it was in the days before television when parents
and children actually talked to each other.
—Andrew H. Malcolm

I know the routine by heart. But does that mean I can't try to do it differently? Car seat, be darned! I know it's for my own protection, but what about my freedom? The straps are too tight and the seat is too low. How am I supposed to view all the cars, trucks, and buses passing by from down here? How am I expected to develop properly if I miss out on what's happening on the streets and highways of this great land? My plaintive wails fall on deaf ears. And wriggling around doesn't work either. It seems there's always someone stronger than me forcing me into this uncomfortable contraption. So for today, I'll take things "one ride at a time." And I'll beep the horn on my way out.

A LITTLE DIRT NEVER HURT

I don't want sundaes, they're too sweet.
And Cheetos are too hard to eat!
I've had my fill of Jell-O, too.
But, wait, I've tasted something new!

Hey, a little dirt never hurt!

Mom says ugh, and makes a face.
But outdoors is my favorite place,
To try all kinds of dirt-filled treats.
Like soil, sand, and bugs—they're neat!

Hey, a little dirt never hurt!

BEHIND THE WHEEL

Just for today, grant me the serenity to get in and out of Daddy's car without touching the steering wheel! Hey, look everybody, I can drive! Look, watch me. I'm going around that hairpin curve. Uh-oh, better slow down. Watch me, watch me. Oops, buckle up, Mom; buckle up, Dad. Hey you, stay in your own lane! Beep-beep, here we go. Speed limit's 55! Hey watch out, buddy! Where'd you learn to drive? Sears?! Whew—that was a close one. Nice blinker, you clown. Okay, we're home. Everybody out! It's my turn to open the garage door. Cool! That was fun. I wanna do it again. Okay, everybody back in the car!

A Meditation

Mom grant me the serenity to trade in
my pacifier for my thumb and blanket.

Mom grant me the serenity to hold my glass with two hands.

Mom grant me the serenity to keep from
grabbing the knife on the table.

Mom grant me the serenity to carry the caterpillar
in the palm of my hand.

Mom grant me the serenity to keep from pulling the cat's tail.

Mom grant me the serenity to stay still while you
use a cold wet wipe on my bottom.

Mom grant me the serenity to keep away from
your toes when riding my tricycle.

Mom grant me the serenity to leave the toys
that don't belong to me at preschool.

Mom grant me the serenity to remember
that I'm not the Mommy.

SHOE FETISH

Sandals, pumps, and espadrilles,
It really is a treat,
To wear Mom's many pairs of shoes,
Upon my little feet.